I0012304

Deep Dive into Orthogonal Persistence

From Theory to Practice

Table of Contents

Chapter 1. Introduction

In this Special Report, we take a comprehensive look at the intricate concept of Orthogonal Persistence, unraveling its mysteries from theory to practical implementation. The subject, though technically sophisticated, will be presented through an approachable dialogue, making it digestible to both the curious novice and the seasoned veteran. We'll journey together from the solid groundwork of the theory, exploring its fundamental principles, right into the heart of its application in real-world scenarios. So fear not, this isn't going to be a mathematical maze. Instead, anticipate a fascinating expedition into the landscape of computer science that fuels much of the digital world we rely on today. Grab ahold of this opportunity, and let's demystify the seemingly intricate world of Orthogonal Persistence together.

Chapter 2. Introduction to Orthogonal Persistence

Orthogonal Persistence, also known as transparent persistence, is one of the most intriguing concepts in the realm of computer science. At its crux, it aims to do away with the artificial line of distinction between primary (volatile) and secondary (non-volatile) storage, thereby offering seamless data management. Intuitively, considering every data bit as persistent implies a world of possibilities. This notion overthrows the traditional concept calling for explicit reading and writing data from and to the storage, thereby working towards simplifying programming models.

2.1. Foundational Understanding

First proposed in a seminal paper by Peter J. Denning in 1978, the concept was further extended by Atkinson, Morrison, Chisholm, and Rosenberg. The term "orthogonal" refers to the separation of concerns, principally between data persistence and the programming model. Concerning Orthogonal Persistence, the data's duration of survival is orthogonal, meaning it is independent of other attributes like the data type or scope.

The major insight behind orthogonal persistence revolves around three key principles: **Process Persistence**, **Data Persistence**, and **Granularity**.

1. **Process Persistence**: In a system supporting process persistence, the process state must prevail across system shutdowns or failures. Restarting the system would result in resuming all the system processes from where they left off.

2. **Data Persistence**: Every piece of data in the system endures until explicitly destroyed. Persistence is not solely a trait of certain

data types or data declared in a particular scope. All data are persistent by default.

3. **Granularity**: Persistence can be applied at different levels - from bit-level granularity to whole systems.

Conceptually, these three principles constitute the foundation of Orthogonal Persistence. They underpin the notion that the lifetime of data and processes isn't limited to the duration of a program, but to the explicit destruction of the given data or process.

2.2. Implementation Strategies

Delving into the practical aspects now, implementing orthogonal persistence involves a multitude of strategies. The strategies range from programming language-level support, through system level support, to the use of separate persistent storage handling modules. Let's discuss these approaches one by one.

1. **Programming Language-level Support**: Some programming languages directly provide features that support data persistence. Languages such as Napier88 or PS-algol were designed from the ground up to natively support persistence.

2. **System-level Support**: Besides language-level persistence, persistence can also be achieved at the system level. Examples of this approach are seen in persistent operating systems such as Grasshopper or Monads.

3. **Separate Persistent Module**: The requirement of persistence can also be achieved without language or system support, by introducing separate modules for handling persistence. Examples of these include database management systems.

Choosing an appropriate strategy depends upon a variety of factors like the size of the system, the persistence ratio (amount of data required to be persistent), system performance requirements and more.

2.3. Persistency in Real World

In the real world, orthogonal persistence has seen application in numerous areas, with database systems being the most common example. Database systems essentially provide a mechanism for secondary storage management and typically involve explicit calls for read and write operations. However, with orthogonal persistence, data manipulation in databases can occur as smoothly as with primary memory variables, without the need for explicit read/write calls.

For instance, consider web developers dealing with backend code. They often spend a significant chunk of their time devising mechanisms for reading from and writing to databases. With orthogonal persistence, this problem is significantly alleviated as the dichotomy between primary and secondary storage management is eliminated.

Another arena where orthogonal persistence has found significant ground is in the context of distributed systems. In distributed systems such as cloud environments, where data needs to be continually available and regularly backed-up, orthogonal persistence plays a vital role.

2.4. Looking Ahead

Orthogonal Persistence, while being a potent concept, is not without its caveats, most notably, the issue of storage space management and garbage collection. With all data being persistent and surviving till explicitly destroyed, efficient mechanisms for managing storage space become critical. Additionally, the persistence of garbage data (users explicitly and deliberately mark as ready for deletion) presents unique challenges.

However, with advancements in technology and need for more adept handling of data, several solutions for these problems are in development.

Orthogonal persistence offers a fresh set of eyes to perceive and interact with data. Its adoption, while demanding changes in conventional programming models, promises to streamline data management, reduce data loss vulnerability, and offer significant leaps towards programmer efficiency.

In conclusion, we embark upon this expedition of understanding with zeal. We'll dive into specific implementations, examine potential advantages, investigate existing pitfalls, and ponder future possibilities offered by Orthogonal Persistence. It's time to swim deeper into the ocean of persistence, so prepare to plunge.

Chapter 3. Theoretical Underpinnings of Orthogonal Persistence

Orthogonal Persistence, a concept embedded in computer science, centers itself on the philosophy of transparent and natural data persistence. Think about numerical data, strings, complex data structures: In a traditional system, you save these explicitly to an external store such as a hard disk, but Orthogonal Persistence aims to make this process seem effortless. The term 'Orthogonal' invariably signifies the notion's goal: to make persistence a separate concern, independent of the whole programming process.

3.1. A Historical Context

The idea of persistent data is not new and was originally explored as part of the Atlas project, a pioneering effort in British computing. The Atlas project introduced a one-level store that transparently kept data persistent through the use of virtual memory. However, the Atlas model fell short of the modern definition of Orthogonal Persistence, as it tightly coupled the lifetime of data with the processes accessing them.

Progressing further, the MONADS project took inspiration from Atlas, enhancing the model by incorporating concepts of object-orientation and capabilites. A defining characteristic of MONADS was that data's lifetime was essentially infinite unless explicitly removed, encapsulating the essence of Orthogonal Persistence.

3.2. Principles of Orthogonal Persistence

Orthogonal Persistence thrives on some key principles that make its implementation possible, essentially focused on two significant aspects: the lifetime of data and transparency.

Firstly, data lifetimes are distinct from the lifespan of processes in Orthogonal Persistence. Unlike conventional systems wherein data disappears as soon as the process generating it terminates, with Orthogonal Persistence data continues to exist indefinitely. It remains persistent until explicitly removed.

Secondly, the transparency of persistent data. Making persistence transparent means the programmer is saved from the hassle of explicitly organizing data import or export from the persistence store. This separation of concerns allows a focus on the core functionality, reducing the complexity of the system overall.

3.3. The Triadic Model

The Triadic Model, proposed by Atkinson and Morrison, nicely encapsulates the principles of Orthogonal Persistence. This model outlines three aspects to be considered orthogonal: the naming of data, the type of data, and the longevity of the data.

The first ties back to the notion of location transparency, incorporated into the design protocol of persistent systems. Here, data is accessed by its identifier regardless of its physical location within the system. Transparency is key and is managed by an orthogonal manager responsible for resource allocation and deallocation.

The data type refers to any data, from the simplest to the complex, treated identically in terms of persistence. This way the system, considering it in an orthogonal perspective, can provide persistent storage even for high-level, user-defined types.

Longevity, as discussed before, corresponds to the lifetime of data, separate from that of the process that creates it. In Orthogonal Persistence, data never dies without explicit removal.

3.4. Orthogonal Persistence Implementation

Implementing Orthogonal Persistence requires careful planning, weighing trade-offs between desired features, and the cost or complexity associated with them. A few approaches have been undertaken, with Persistent Programming Languages (PPLs) leading the way. Indeed, PPLs such as PS-Algol and Napier88 have been explicit free moving through coding, data handling, and execution, embedding the principles of persistence inherently into the language syntax and semantics.

Another approach for implementation includes file mapping, which is straightforward, leveraging the operating system's virtual memory manager to map files onto memory. However, this technique tends to be more - and unnecessarily - complex due to issues in type checking and garbage collection.

Over the recent years, Object databases and Object-Relational mapping (OR-Mapping) tools have gained traction in the arena of Orthogonal Persistence. These tools encapsulate persistence functions within object methods permitting effortless management and manipulation of persistent data.

It's crucial to note that no one-size-fits-all solution exists for implementing Orthogonal Persistence. The choice of technique solely depends on the needs of the application, the existing environment and the preferences of the system architect.

Orthogonal Persistence, though powerful in its objectives, is weighed down by a slew of challenges. It can lead to complicated debugging and testing, and impose performance overheads due to the required transparency. However, with continued innovation and exploration, we can aim for a future where program data's persistence is as natural as the persistence of objects in our everyday world.

In conclusion, the theoretical foundations of Orthogonal Persistence lie in its objective to keep data persisting 'naturally' and 'transparently'. Its principles, deeply tied with the concepts of data lifetimes and transparency, are intuitively encapsulated in the Triadic Model. While its implementation incurs a set of challenges and trade-offs, the benefits of such a system greatly facilitate the tasks of the programmer. Despite its complex surface, Orthogonal Persistence is a fascinating delve into the intricacies of data handling in computer systems.

Chapter 4. Orthogonal vs. Non-Orthogonal Persistence: A Comparative Study

Orthogonal persistence and non-orthogonal persistence reside as two polarities on the persistence spectrum. As we dive deeper into this comparative study, we will reveal different aspects of these methodologies, their variances, and where each one finds its merits and holds its challenges.

4.1. Understanding Orthogonal Persistence

Orthogonal persistence refers to the idea that data in a program continues to exist even after the termination of the program. This persistence is considered "orthogonal", or unchanging, as it doesn't rely on the programmer to manually save and load data - it's an automatic process.

Let's consider a simple analogy to better understand this. Imagine running your favorite video game on your computer. You're in the middle of a particularly hectic level when suddenly there's a power cut. Naturally, you'd be frustrated. But when the power returns, you find that upon restarting the game, you are right back where you left off, all your in-game progress retained. This is orthogonal persistence in action - the data was preserved, or persisted, despite the abrupt termination of the program (in this case, the game).

In a more formal setting, a system with orthogonal persistence would inherently oversee processes so that objects produced during a computation are preserved between uses of the program. Programmers then can focus on the computational problem at hand, rather than the additional, tangential problem of how to ensure data persistence.

4.2. Dealing with Non-Orthogonal Persistence

In direct contrast, non-orthogonal persistence relies heavily on the explicit actions of the programmer to preserve data beyond the lifetime of a program. The programmer manually delineates what data is stored, where the data should be stored, and when it should be saved or loaded. Due to the specificity and control the programmer has, non-orthogonal persistence finds its usage in scenarios where certain aspects of data need to be safeguarded more stringently than others, or where the process and timing of data preservation need to be precisely controlled.

To return to our previous metaphor, in the non-orthogonal persistence scenario, if the power cut occurs while you're in the middle of your game, when the power returns and the game is restarted, all progress since the last save point would be lost. However, the information saved up until the last save point, as instructed by the player (or programmer, in real-world scenarios), would persist.

4.3. The Theoretical Contrast

The broad difference in these approaches is their fundamental philosophical distinction. Orthogonal persistence is conceptually simple, lending it elegance. It focuses on the principle that data should naturally survive the lifespan of the process that creates it.

On the other hand, non-orthogonal persistence gives the programmer complete control over the data's persistence. This extra control can make this approach attractive for some applications but also places a greater responsibility on the programmer.

4.4. Comparative Analysis: Memory and Processing Overheads

Orthogonal persistence requires continuous monitoring of changing data, which invariably leads to increased memory and processing overhead. The system must remain vigilant and keep track of the data in real time. This can result in a slower runtime, especially in programs that deal with high volumes of mutable data.

Contrarily, non-orthogonal persistence only incurs overhead when the programmer calls for data to be saved or loaded. This offers significant processing power and memory savings, as unused or unimportant data does not need to be persisted just because it happened to be in existence during the program's runtime.

4.5. Comparison: Error Recovery and Data Consistency

Orthogonal persistence shines when it comes to error recovery and data consistency. Since all data is continuously saved, data loss due to unexpected crashes or errors is minimized, enhancing data integrity. It also makes rollbacks or recovering previous states more accessible, as every state change is recorded.

Non-orthogonal persistence does not offer these benefits directly because data is saved only upon explicit instructions. However, it could be leveraged with additional error recovery mechanisms implemented by the programmer.

4.6. Evaluation: Programmer's Control and Flexibility

With non-orthogonal persistence, the programmer has much better control over what gets stored, when, and where. This can be a real asset when dealing with sensitive or confidential information that should not always be automatically saved. It also provides the flexibility to optimize for speed and efficiency, as extraneous data can be excluded from the saving process.

Orthogonal persistence, although elegant and straightforward in its approach, may not always offer the flexibility required in more complex or sensitive contexts.

Chapter 5. The Verdict: Orthogonal vs Non-Orthogonal Persistence

The battle of orthogonal versus non-orthogonal persistence is not about determining an overall winner. Instead, it's about understanding these strategies, their strengths and weaknesses, and discerning where to apply them for the best results. Problems with different contexts and constraints will benefit from these methods to varying degrees. Hence, the choice between orthogonal and non-orthogonal persistence depends ultimately on the unique requirements and characteristics of the task at hand. The aim should be to strike a balance yielding maximum benefit for the specific given scenario while mitigating potential downsides.

Chapter 6. Breaking Down the Persistence Spectrum

Orthogonal Persistence, at its core, can be thought of as a property of a system - whether it be a programming language, a data store, or an entire operating system - that allows data created during an execution to continue to exist even after that execution is complete. But to truly appreciate the importance and the complexity of this concept, we need to delve deeper into the Persistence Spectrum, a continuum that showcases the various degrees and forms in which persistence can exist.

To envision the Persistence Spectrum, picture a wide continuum, with Temporary Persistence at one end and Orthogonal Persistence at the other. Understanding each point along this spectrum, its unique features, and how they each fit into the bigger picture of Persistence, will allow us to truly grasp the concept of Orthogonal Persistence.

6.1. The Shallow End: Temporary Persistence

Temporary Persistence is the base of the Persistence Spectrum, seemingly simple in its function, yet vital in the grand scheme of things. This is what we see in typical programming languages where data exists only for the duration of the execution. The variables we define, the values we assign, they live only as long as the program runs. After that, they disappear, wiped clean. This is Temporary Persistence.

At this point in the spectrum, there is certainly persistence, but it's not the kind we're focusing on. This form of persistence is fleeting, like the minimal viable definition of persistence; the data merely doesn't vanish the moment it comes into existence.

Along with providing a foundation of understanding, Temporary Persistence sets up the scene for the exploration of more complex forms of Persistence.

6.2. The Transition: Manual Persistence

Manual Persistence acts as a bridge between the simplicity of Temporary Persistence and the complexity of the remaining spectrum. It involves deliberately saving data to an external file or a database to make it persist beyond the execution time.

A good example of Manual Persistence in action is when we create a text file to note down values that a program produces. The programmer ensures the Persistent behavior in this case, but this still isn't quite Orthogonal Persistence. While data is preserved across executions, it requires explicit instruction - a manual save command for each piece of data we wish to persist.

However, Manual Persistence is not explicit to file systems; it also includes databases where data can exist independent of whether the program that wrote the data is running or not. From a developer's perspective, the use of such systems marks a shift towards the desire for more persistent solutions.

6.3. Long-Term Persistence: Durable Transient Systems

Durable Transient Systems mark the deeper end of the Persistence Spectrum. Here, persistence spans across multiple executions and data isn't lost even when machines power on and off. Database management systems, disks, and tapes used for data storage are perfect examples.

These systems constantly save data as it is produced, and in case of hard disks or tapes, the data is often written almost immediately to persistent storage. To a user, the entire system might appear to be Orthogonally Persistent, as their data persists across various operations. However, these are not truly Orthogonally Persistent as they are not automatic and transparent.

6.4. The Deep End: Orthogonal Persistence

At the farthest end of the Persistence Spectrum, we encounter Orthogonal Persistence. This is where data persists across executions transparently and automatically - without explicit instructions to store or retrieve data. Memory or data persistence in this model is orthogonal to execution time; data continues to exist, from one process to the next, without any direct commands from the programmer to save or load it.

Orthogonal Persistence offers a higher level of abstraction in programming models - the hassle of managing lifetime or validity of data objects is taken away from the programmer, making their work more intuitive.

In this kind of system, the persistence of data isn't the programmer's concern. This doesn't just bring more simplicity and elegance to the code but also leads to more reliable and less error-prone programming, as there are fewer chances for mistakes related to mishandling of data lifetimes.

Chapter 7. Conclusion

The journey along the Persistence Spectrum takes us through progressively more complex and efficient forms of data persistence. The ultimate goal of any persistence model is to provide reliable, convenient, and efficient means of storing data, and as we traverse the spectrum from Temporary Persistence to Orthogonal Persistence, we see exactly how this evolves.

Understanding the Persistence Spectrum is tantamount to understand Orthogonal Persistence. With this understanding, we can begin to dive deeper into the fascinating, intricate structures of Orthogonal Persistence itself. As we step closer to the edge of the Persistence Spectrum, we inch closer to making our analytical expedition to understand the world of Orthogonal Persistence, more enlightening and complete.

Chapter 8. Programming Models for Orthogonal Persistence

Orthogonal Persistence - a concept that decouples the lifecycle of the data from the processes manipulating it - has paved the way towards efficient handling of persistent data in computing. Under the hood of this intriguing concept lie numerous programming models that provide a structural framework to enable its proper assimilation into application design and execution.

The selection of an effective model for Orthogonal Persistence depends upon various factors such as the design, complexity, and computing environment of the application. Our focus in this chapter is to provide a detailed study on these programming models and discuss how each one can be implementated pragmatically.

8.1. Reachability-Based Programming Model

The reachability-based model of Orthogonal Persistence is predicated on the reachability of an object in memory from the root of the program. When a process is executed, all the objects that can be reached are made persistent. This model sprouts directly from the theory of Orthogonal Persistence, where any data created during a process persists beyond the lifespan of the process itself.

This programming model offers the advantage of simplicity but may lead to potentially unwanted data being stored persistently. Thus, while opting for this model, developers should stay mindful of unintended reachability, which could bloat the persistent data.

8.2. The Transactional Programming Model

The transactional model for Orthogonal Persistence operates on the principle of 'transactions'. A transaction refers to a series of operations bundled together as a single, indivisible unit. This model commits or reverts all changes made during a transaction, ensuring that the persistent state is always consistent.

The transactional model offers strong consistency guarantees and safeguards against potential data corruption. However, it necessitates careful planning to maintain optimal performance, especially in high-load scenarios, given the overhead of managing transaction conflicts.

8.3. Checkpoint-Based Programming Model

In the checkpoint-based model, Orthogonal Persistence is achieved by taking a 'snapshot' or checkpoint of the application state at specified intervals. Like an ongoing diary of status updates, these checkpoints hold all information about the state of the process, allowing one to revert back to a particular state if needed.

This model provides robustness and flexibility but can be resource-intensive, particularly for applications with a large state. Therefore, strategies for intelligent checkpointing minimizing the performance impact should be considered.

8.4. The Generational Programming Model

The generational model of orthogonal persistence inherits ideas from generational garbage collection techniques. The basic idea is to divide data into different 'generations' or tiers based on the time when they were created or last used. As time goes by, the data not accessed recently is considered 'old' and moved to a lower tier. Eventually, the data in the lower tiers moves to the persistent storage.

This model aims to keep the most frequently accessed data in memory, boosting program efficiency. However, the complexity associated with the maintenance of 'generations' can be a potential downside of this model.

8.5. Model Comparison and Selecting the Right Model

Orthogonal Persistence is a powerful tool to achieve data persistence, and the choice of the programming model can significantly influence its performance and efficiency. The comparison and selection of the right model are based on fulfilling the requirements of the application.

The reachability-based model offers simplicity and is appropriate for memory-based persistence where data volume is not a concern. The transactional model ensures strong consistency, making it suitable for financial and banking sectors where data consistency holds paramount importance.

The checkpoint-based model is ideal for applications where fault tolerance is the priority, like high-performance computing applications where the cost of failure is high. The generational model can be a fit for systems where data is accessed unevenly, and it's essential to keep the most accessed data close to the CPU.

Choosing one model over the other is a delicate balance of trade-offs. The decision would entail an analysis of the application's nature, the volume of data to handle, and the computational resources available. With these considerations, we can select the right programming model to employ Orthogonal Persistence in the most effective and efficient way.

As this explanation concludes, we hope that the maze-like concept of programming models for Orthogonal Persistence is a bit less cryptic. Indeed, their smart implementation in real-world scenarios can make a significant impact on the performance and effectiveness of software systems.

In our next dive, we will unravel the intricacies of implementing these models inside popular programming languages, so stay on board as we continue our exploration of the world of Orthogonal Persistence.

Chapter 9. Implementing Orthogonal Persistence: Practical Case Studies

As we dive into the practical implementation of Orthogonal Persistence, we start at the core - the API design. This, as much as it's simplified in implementation, can carry the most weight in the feasibility of maintaining persistence.

9.1. The Importance of API design

With Orthogonal Persistence, it's crucial that application programming interfaces (APIs) support the overarching objectives of persistence. They should encapsulate resources, providing clear, concise methods for interaction. The programming model should remain as constant as possible, reducing the burden placed on developers.

This means that APIs need to be transparent, in that the details of how data is accessed and stored are abstracted away from the programmer. All objects should be treated equally, regardless of their lifetime or eventual destination (memory, disk, etc.).

A good strategy is to implement a copy-on-write system. When an application modifies an object, a copy of the object is created specifically for that application, while the original object remains unaltered. If an application creates an object and doesn't modify it, no data is written, which saves on unnecessary disk I/O.

9.2. Persistence Libraries

Persistence libraries can save developers a great deal of work by providing a transparent or near-transparent interface for handling persistent objects in memory. They provide a number of services, such as:

- Opening and defending resources
- Locking objects for concurrency control
- Interacting with garbage collection mechanisms
- Load-time class replacement

Java's attempt at persistence is JDBC. The Java version of this persistence paradigm also includes an API for object-relational mapping, facilitating data storage in a more raw, relatable format.

9.3. Dirty Bits and Infrastructure

Dirty bits are a simple practical technique used to identify changed objects for write-back to disk. A 'dirty bit' is a flag that is set when an object is written to, signaling the need for it to be written back to disk. This infrastructure makes it feasible to implement the 'copy on write' strategy above.

Java and C, among others, have implemented such a system, enabling objects to be serialized to, and from, the persistent store. Some implementations also use smart pointers, such as those provided by Boost in C, to transparently manage these objects, and their various states across memory and disk.

9.4. Persistence in Distributed Systems

Persistence comes into complicated play when considering distributed systems. The requirements of data replication for fault tolerance, up and consistent network latency, and user demand for speed all come into clash. The volatile nature of network connections must be taken into account when we deal with the problem of distributed system persistence.

One popular solution is a distributed filesystem, which simplifies the model by presenting it to the system as local storage. Examples include Google's Bigtable and Amazon's Dynamo, which offer high scalability and consistency in the face of network partitions. A distributed system could, theoretically, build upon these systems to provide a persistent, standardized interface for developers.

In summary, implementing Orthogonal Persistence in the real world means having to deal with a host of issues beyond object lifespan. Distributed systems add an extra layer of complexity. However, clever design of APIs, use of libraries and recognition of the importance of infrastructure such as 'dirty bits', can ease developers' burdens in managing persistence and result in effective solutions that align with the principles of Orthogonal Persistence. With this in practice, we can better handle the deluge of data characterizing our digital world.

Chapter 10. Challenges and Opportunities in Orthogonal Persistence

Orthogonal Persistence, though a vital component in system robustness, presents its unique set of challenges, which instigate innovative solutions. Coupled with the challenges come an array of opportunities that potentially revolutionize software design and data management.

10.1. Defining the Challenges

A deep dive into the world of Orthogonal Persistence necessitates an understanding of the challenges that surround its implementation. This knowledge serves to inspire solutions that make for iteratively robust systems.

The complexity of persistence management is perhaps the most significant hurdle. Architecting a system where every action, function, or procedure is intrinsically intertwined with persistence requires a substantial shift in the conventional application design mindset.

Another significant hurdle is the sheer volume of persistent data generated by such systems. As every action, irrespective of its significance in the larger context, leads to data creation, the amount of data that needs to be handled can quickly spiral out of control. Efficient data management becomes crucial, not only to prevent system slow down, but also to ward off storage bottlenecks.

Last, but hardly the least, is the challenge of backward compatibility. As systems continually evolve, persistence architectures have a responsibility to uphold the integrity of pre-existing data --a task that can quickly become complex with major system shifts.

10.2. The Opportunities Lying Ahead

However daunting these challenges appear, they carry with them a silver lining of opportunities to foster innovation in the field of software design and data management.

Orthogonal Persistence can inspire a rethinking of conventional application design. Although this process requires a paradigm shift for programmers, it presents a remarkable opportunity for streamlining system functions. By eliminating the need for explicit save or load functions, the system's workflow could be vastly improved leading to a more intuitive and seamless user experience.

Another upside to Orthogonal Persistence is the possibility of superior data recovery capabilities. As each operation, down to minutest detail, is perpetually stored, systems can have the ability to recover from any point of failure. This trait can greatly increase software robustness, reducing the possibility of catastrophic failures.

Finally, the challenge of handling voluminous data has a bright side. It nudges the data storage and management industry to come up with better solutions for data efficiency. This challenge drives innovation, leading to improved storage mediums and optimization algorithms that improve not just Orthogonal Persistence-backed systems, but data handling overall.

10.3. Addressing Challenges: Realizing the Paradigm Shift

The inherent complexity in managing persistence needs a shift in the mindset of programmers. They must learn to weave persistence seamlessly into all aspects of system function, rather than treating it as an after-thought or a feature to be bolted on later.

There are also the considerations of synchronicity and immediacy in persistence that come into play here. Should every operation in a system be immediately and synchronously persisted? Or should there be an optimal balance, based on the criticality of operations? These are decisions to be made consciously, and clearly defined policies to be implemented for these decisions which demand a higher degree of architectural planning and foresight from the developers' end.

10.4. Handling Data Voluminous

As Orthogonal Persistence can lead to the creation of extensive data, devising efficient data management solutions is essential. This calls for the application of techniques like regular pruning or archives of irrelevant data. Sophisticated algorithms could be utilized for determining what constitutes as vital data, and what qualifies as non-essential, thereby making data handling more efficient.

Simultaneously, the need to handle larger volumes of data can push storage mediums to increase capacities and optimize their performance. This aspect could encourage the growth of cloud-based solutions or advancement in physical storage technologies.

10.5. Upholding Backward Compatibility

Maintaining backward compatibility with pre-existing data is a crucial aspect of a persistence architecture. However, applying version control to persistence mechanics, albeit challenging, can offer an excellent solution to this problem.

Systems need to be resilient enough to accommodate changes while preserving access to, and usage of, legacy data. This could involve the application of complex versioning solutions that maintain a track of, and adapt to, system developments over time.

The journey to implementing a robust Orthogonal Persistence system is a challenging one. It calls for a paradigm shift in design thinking, efficient data management, and backward compatibility. However, these challenges illuminate the path for remarkable opportunities in the fields of software design and data management. With the right approach, these opportunities can be leveraged to foster innovation and build systems that exhibit a higher standard of robustness and user experience.

Chapter 11. Orthogonal Persistence in Database Systems

Orthogonal Persistence is an influential concept that impinges various aspects of computing, with database systems being one of the principal beneficiaries. In the essence of achieving a robust and efficient database system, this concept lays the foundation for ensuring data persistence in a uniform and systematic manner.

11.1. Understanding Orthogonal Persistence

Persistence, in the context of data management, refers to the characteristic of data, outliving the process that created it. In other words, it's the capability to store data structures in non-volatile storage systems like a database, so they can be retrieved and reused in upcoming executions.

The concept of Orthogonal Persistence extends the basic notion of persistence to encompass every object on a system, regardless of its runtime lifespan. It's "orthogonal" because it's independent of any data type or storage object — a universal, all-embracing characteristic.

11.2. The Principles of Orthogonal Persistence

Orthogonal persistence is guided by three main principles, which form the keystone of its implementation:

1. **The Principle of Persistence Independence:** The persistence or transience of an object should not affect its design. Whether an object is persistent or transient should be incidental and not a key part of its identity.

2. **The Persistence Identification Principle:** This principle suggests the decision to make an object persistent or transient should be made at the level of individual objects rather than at the aggregated granularity of a program or system.

3. **The Principle of Orthogonality:** All objects are treated uniformly regarding persistence, irrespective of the complexity or simplicity of their data types.

This set of principles ensures a smooth and efficient way of managing data, providing both the developers and users of a system with a framework that balances comprehensiveness, simplicity, and efficiency.

11.3. Database Systems and Orthogonal Persistence

The interconnection of database systems and the concept of Orthogonal Persistence unveils a symbiotic relationship. When implemented properly, this principle could bring about radical improvements in the realm of data persistence and management.

To start with, let's analyze how this concept brings universality to persistence. It allows for the automatic persistence of all objects in a system, irrespective of their data type or methods they're involved with. This feature is advantageous for large-scale systems where the manual marking of persistent objects can be prone to errors or often intractable.

Furthermore, Orthogonal Persistence could substantially reduce redundancies, increase program simplification, and boost the overall performance of a system.

11.4. Implementing Orthogonal Persistence

Even though the benefits of implementing this concept are notable, the task is often inundated with challenges. It's mostly due to the requirement of memory management, garbage collection, and consistency maintenance in a persistent context.

The following represents potential solutions for implementing the concept:

1. **Persistent Programming Languages:** Languages like Napier88 and PS-algol were explicitly designed to support orthogonal persistence. They provide syntactic constructs, semantics, and runtime support that mark and manage persistent data directly within the programming language.

2. **Persistent Operating Systems:** These types of systems, like Grasshopper, offer support for Orthogonal Persistence at the OS level.

3. **Persistent Object Stores:** Solutions such as PJama provide a storage layer that offers persistence support for common programming languages without requiring language or OS support.

11.5. Challenges and Advancements

Despite its potential benefits, Orthogonal Persistence implementation is not without its set of challenges. Issues related to system complexity, performance overheads, and security risks call for innovative solutions and continuous advancements in this field.

One significant advancement is the use of Shadow Paging, a disk-oriented technique, which helps enhance system performance by avoiding in-place updates of persistent data.

In contemporary development, the merging of imminent technologies like Blockchain with the principles of Orthogonal Persistence sights a promising perspective. Blockchain, with its inherent immutability and distributed ledger, can sustain orthogonal persistence in new, secure ways, providing exciting avenues for future investigation.

As we keep pushing the boundaries of data management, the principles of Orthogonal Persistence continue to remain relevant. The drive is towards an era where its implementation becomes increasingly seamless, serving as the backbone for virtually every type of computer system. Through continuous efforts in research and development, we can begin to demystify the concept, making it more accessible and putting it to use in ways we've just begun to explore.

Chapter 12. Future Predictions: Advancements in Orthogonal Persistence

In the realm of computing, Orthogonal Persistence stands tall as a profound concept that has shaped the course of engineering of modern systems. Its utility is widely recognized, with applications spanning from data management to programming languages and beyond. Is it then possible to envision a future that leaps beyond the current capabilities? The answer is a resounding yes.

12.1. The Potentials and Realities of Quantum Computing

Ponder, if you will, the realm of quantum computing where qubits defy the traditional binary constraints, existing in multiple states at once. Orthogonal Persistence in this dimension can unlock a whole new realm of solutions. The delicacy of quantum memory, with its superposed state, can benefit from a persistent environment. Though the reality of quantum computing is still in its infancy, the seed has been planted, and with careful nurturing, this concept can take root and eventually blossom.

The integration of Orthogonal Persistence with quantum computing would allow an application's state to survive crashes and unexpected halts. Thus, resulting in the possibility of applications that not only offer computational prowess but also unprecedented reliability. Transplanting the principles of Orthogonal Persistence into the quantum computing landscape, although a deep dive into uncharted waters right now, holds the potential to become a reality soon, reinventing not just the future of computing altogether, but also the future of persistence.

12.2. Artificial Intelligence - Redefining Persistence

Artificial Intelligence (AI) has been a playground for innovation in the tech industry. Orthogonal Persistence, although not a directly contributing factor to comprehend AI, has strong implications concerning the permanence of learning and adaptable AI systems.

Consider an AI application which learns, adapts, and evolves with time. When it halts or a crash occurs, the learned knowledge would be lost in traditional systems. Orthogonal Persistence, therefore, becomes a beacon of hope to maintain the knowledge of the AI systems persistently.

It's the persistence of learned knowledge that will potentially change the way AI systems are developed and operated. The crossroad between AI and Orthogonal Persistence, though filled with technical complexities, promises a future enriched by intelligent systems packed with enduring comprehension.

12.3. Augmented and Virtual Reality - The Persistence of Experience

Augmented and Virtual Reality (AR & VR) technologies blend digital and physical worlds to provide immersive experiences. The future of these technologies intertwined with Orthogonal Persistence becomes overwhelmingly exciting. Imagine a VR application allowing a realistic walk in a digital world holding your progress and interactions persistently.

As AR & VR technologies enhance personal experiences, persistence can play a pivotal role in tracking these experiences and maintaining continuous interactions over multiple sessions. The future landscape of AR & VR, blessed by the divine touch of Orthogonal Persistence, promises a world where experiences persist over time and space, causing a paradigm shift in the immersive technologies panorama.

12.4. Comprehensive Data Management Systems

Data has become the lifeblood of the digital age. And with Orthogonal Persistence, we have a powerful tool in our arsenal to manage it more effectively. We can foresee a future where comprehensive data management systems employ this concept extensively to streamline operations and ensure data integrity.

In such futuristic data management systems, databases won't be an isolated entity requiring separate backups for maintaining data. Instead, they will morph into an integral part of applications, holding and preserving the data state persistently. This future offers a tantalizing vista of databases naturally possessed with resilience, efficiency, and a new level of reliability.

12.5. Simplifying Programming Languages

Orthogonal Persistence is not just about maintenance of data states, but it also has promising prospects in making programming languages simpler and more efficient. The future holds the prospects of programming languages with built-in support for persistence, eliminating the requirement of implementing explicit file opening, reading, writing, and closing operations.

This would give rise to an environment where persistence is a basic property of any data structure, therefore simplifying and enhancing the programming culture by a significant degree, promoting the development of robust and resilient applications while reducing the complexity and codes lines.

In conclusion, the course of Orthogonal Persistence's journey is expected to take several unforeseen turns. Each one will unveil a new horizon enhancing not just one or two dimensions of computing but remolding multiple aspects altogether. With quantum computing, artificial intelligence, augmented and virtual reality, comprehensive data management systems, and innovative programming languages models, Orthogonal Persistence contributes to creating a future where the virtual world becomes more consistent, enduring, and reliable. Prepare to embrace a future where persistence has expanded its circle from system designs to everyday computing experiences.

Chapter 13. Wrapping Up: Key Takeaways from the Orthogonal Persistence Journey

We've traveled an extensive journey together, from understanding the foundational principles of Orthogonal Persistence (also referred to as just "Persistence" henceforth) to diving neck-deep into real-world applications. It's time to draw together the threads of what we've learned, solidify our comprehension, and understand the significance of this computer science concept on a more profound level.

13.1. The Foundation: Remembering the Essentials

Fundamentally, Persistence is all about maintaining the state of a program despite interruptions. This capability allows computer systems to retain data across multiple executions, enabling users to power down and resume their work without data loss or disruption.

It's important to clarify that the notion of Persistence isn't synonymous with simple data storage. The essence really lies in remembering the 'state' of an application. Like waking up from a night of deep sleep and continuing the previous day's tasks exactly where you left off without missing a beat.

Think of Persistence as the thread stitching together
the two separate executions of a program, making them
appear continuous. This thread, when carefully woven
into the fabric of software, can significantly enhance
the user experience.

13.2. Orthogonality: A Touch of Mathematical Precision

Orthogonality, the other half of our complex term,
injects a layer of elegance and precision into the mix.
In mathematics, orthogonal elements are independent or
non-interfering, drawing parallels to our subject
matter.

In the context of Persistence, orthogonality implies
that the mechanisms used to achieve Persistence do not
interfere with, or depend on the main program
functionality. This noninterference allows programming
and Persistence concerns to be handled separately, which
is a boon for software engineering processes.

13.3. Integrated Approaches: The Marriage of Program State and Persistence

There are two main integrated approaches used to achieve Orthogonal Persistence – persistence by reachability and persistence by designation.

Persistence by reachability regards any data reachable from a root as persistent. This approach ensures that all related data gets preserved across program executions, making it an intuitive choice for many programming contexts.

Meanwhile, persistence by designation explicitly tags certain data as persistent. This gives developers more control over what state gets remembered, limiting persistence to critical pieces of data and reducing unnecessary storage.

Both methods carry their advantages and inherent limitations, guiding developers in selecting the best-suited style for their specific software systems.

13.4. Implementing Orthogonal Persistence: Techniques and Technologies

Adding Orthogonal Persistence to a program requires a mix of well-chosen technologies and careful design decisions. Here are a few key concepts worth revisiting:

- File systems: The most basic mechanism for adding persistence. But they require explicit and continuous developer involvement.

- Databases: Provides a higher level of abstraction and ease of use compared to file systems. However, objects often need to be broken down into relational data.

- Object databases: Objects don't need deconstruction and reconstruction, providing a good match for object-oriented languages. Yet, adoption is less widespread due to complexity and the prevalence of relational databases.

- Object-relational mapping (ORM) tools: Bridge the gap between object-oriented programs and relational databases. Considerations include learning curve, potential for performance bottlenecks, and introducing complexity.

- Previous System Pointers (PSPs): Highlights the advantage of Orthogonality, providing a single reference point to resume program execution.

13.5. Impacts: Reshaping the Digital Landscape

Orthogonal Persistence has broad ramifications across

technology, influencing areas like databases, operating systems, and high-level programming languages. It is shaping our digital landscape, affecting everything from the user experience of general software, to critical systems like healthcare and finance applications.

13.6. Future Directions: Adapting to a Changing World

The journey into Orthogonal Persistence isn't complete without acknowledging its promising future. As technology charges forward, new challenges, medium constraints, and use-cases for Persistence continue to emerge.

Keep an eye out for improving performance, simplifying implementations, and reducing the cognitive load for developers. The goal is to make Orthogonal Persistence an even more seamless part of modern software engineering.

The tantalizing notion of 'Ubiquitous Persistence' paints a picture of future software systems where Persistence is the default, and data loss due to system failures becomes a relic of the past.

13.7. Wrapping Up

Indeed, stepping into the realm of Orthogonal

Persistence reveals a rich tapestry of techniques, concepts, challenges, and triumphs. This journey offers us far more than just a theoretical understanding. It empowers us, as developers and aspirants, with the understanding required to design more robust, user-friendly, and innovative software. It helps us appreciate how a seemingly obscure mathematical concept can notably fashion the digital world. Much like an enjoyable voyage, the memories made along this journey are as valuable as the final destination. After all, an expedition into the landscape of computer science is complete only when we can take those lessons and apply them to the canvas of our digital world, creating vibrant, resilient, and enduring systems.

www.ingramcontent.com/pod-product-compliance
Lightning Source LLC
LaVergne TN
LVHW051624050326
832903LV00033B/4657